Roberto Clemente

A LIFE OF GENEROSITY

by Sheila Anderson

PULL AHEAD Biographies

Lerner Publications Company • Minneapolis

Photo Acknowledgments

The images in this book are used with the permission of: © Bettmann/CORBIS, pp. 4, 14, 15, 20, 22; The Art Archive/Culver Pictures, p. 6; © Three Lions/Hulton Archive/Getty Images, pp. 7, 18; © Thomas D. McAvoy/Time & Life Pictures/Getty Images, p. 8; AP Photo/John McConnico, p. 9; Library of Congress, p. 10 (LC-DIG-fsac-1a34013); © Photo File/MLB Photos via Getty Images, p. 12; National Baseball Hall of Fame Library, Cooperstown, N.Y., pp. 16, 17, 25; © Gordon Parks/Time & Life Pictures/Getty Images, p. 19; © Michael Ochs Archives/Getty Images, p. 21; AP Photo, p. 24; © Rich Pilling/MLB Photos via Getty Images, p. 26.

Front Cover: AP Photo.

Lerner Publications Company
A division of Lerner Publishing Group, Inc.
241 First Avenue North
Minneapolis, MN 55401 U.S.A.

Website address: www.lernerbooks.com

Words in **bold type** are explained in a glossary on page 31.

Library of Congress Cataloging-in-Publication Data

Anderson, Sheila.
    Roberto Clemente : a life of generosity / by Sheila Anderson.
      p.   cm. — (Pull ahead books. Biographies)
    Includes index.
    ISBN-13: 978-0-8225-8586-2 (lib. bdg. : alk. paper)
    1. Clemente, Roberto, 1934–1972—Juvenile literature. 2. Baseball players—Puerto Rico—Biography—Juvenile literature. 3. Generosity—Juvenile literature. I. Title.
    GV865.C45 A63 2008
    796.357092—dc22 [B]   2007013531

Manufactured in the United States of America
1 2 3 4 5 6 – JR – 13 12 11 10 09 08

Table of Contents

Roberto Clemente

Baseball Beginnings

Pow! A soup can flies through the air.
A boy runs across a dusty field. He
tries to catch the can. He misses.
Another can shoots toward the sky.
The boy hitting these cans is Roberto
Clemente. He dreams of becoming a
professional baseball player.

Roberto Clemente was born in 1934. He lived with his family in Puerto Rico. Puerto Rico is an island in the Caribbean Sea.

Roberto grew up near San Juan, Puerto Rico.

Kids play baseball in Puerto Rico, about 1940.

Roberto loved to play baseball. It
didn't matter that he did not have a
baseball or a bat.

Roberto and his friends used cans or tied up rags for baseballs.

Many kids in Puerto Rico played games with things they found outside.

A boy plays stickball with his friends.

They used a tree branch or a piece of wood for a bat.

Sometimes, Roberto worked with his father in sugarcane fields like this one.

Helping at Home

Roberto was a good ball player. He was also a **generous** boy. He did small jobs to help earn money for his family. Roberto's parents taught him to help others too.

12

Giving to Others

When Roberto was eighteen years old, he started playing professional baseball in Puerto Rico. Then, his big chance came. A team in the United States wanted him to play there. In 1955, he joined the Pittsburgh Pirates.

Roberto became a popular player. But he never forgot the lessons his parents taught him about being generous.

Roberto always had time for his fans.

Roberto and his mother

Roberto earned a lot of money playing baseball. But he was not **selfish**. He bought his parents a new house.

When he wasn't playing baseball, Roberto went home to Puerto Rico.

Roberto owned a farm in Carolina, Puerto Rico.

Roberto traveled around Puerto Rico.
He taught children about baseball.

He talked to them about being good **citizens**. He also visited children in hospitals.

Roberto spoke to children like these in Puerto Rico.

Roberto wanted to do something special for poor children in Puerto Rico.

He planned to build a sports center there. It would be a place where kids could come to learn and play sports.

Roberto enjoyed teaching kids about baseball.

Roberto wanted kids to have a safe place to play sports, such as volleyball.

Roberto's sports center would be free for all children.

A Generous End

In 1972, an **earthquake** shook the country of **Nicaragua**. Buildings fell down. Many people died. Roberto wanted to help the people there. He collected money and food. He helped load trucks and planes with clothing and medicines.

Roberto decided to go to Nicaragua. He wanted to make sure people got the supplies they needed.

Workers gave food and supplies to people in Nicaragua.

The airplane Roberto rode in crashed. Roberto died. People all over the world were sad.

This award is given each year to a baseball player who helps others the way Roberto did.

Wish Come True

Roberto's family knew about his plans to make a sports center in Puerto Rico. They built the center. They named it Roberto Clemente Sports City. Stadiums, schools, and bridges have also been named for Roberto Clemente. People still remember his generosity.

ROBERTO CLEMENTE TIMELINE

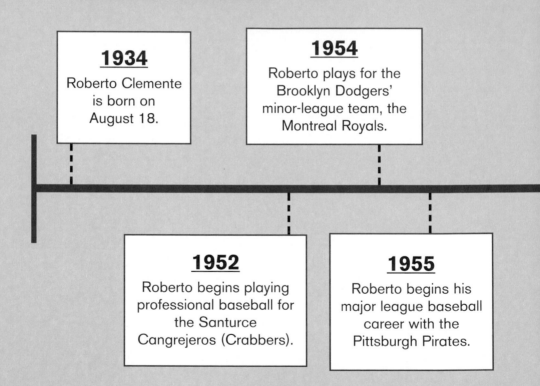

1934
Roberto Clemente is born on August 18.

1954
Roberto plays for the Brooklyn Dodgers' minor-league team, the Montreal Royals.

1952
Roberto begins playing professional baseball for the Santurce Cangrejeros (Crabbers).

1955
Roberto begins his major league baseball career with the Pittsburgh Pirates.

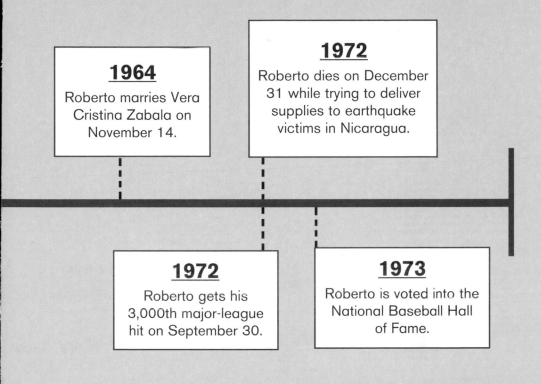

1964
Roberto marries Vera Cristina Zabala on November 14.

1972
Roberto dies on December 31 while trying to deliver supplies to earthquake victims in Nicaragua.

1972
Roberto gets his 3,000th major-league hit on September 30.

1973
Roberto is voted into the National Baseball Hall of Fame.

More about Roberto Clemente

● Roberto chose the number 21 to wear on his jersey because his full name, Roberto Clemente Walker, has 21 letters.

● In 1973, the Commissioner's Award was renamed the Roberto Clemente Award. Each year, it is given to a major league baseball player who demonstrates sportsmanship, good character, and community involvement.

● Roberto's family created the Roberto Clemente Foundation. It helps teenagers in Pittsburgh, Pennsylvania, through sports and educational programs.

Websites

Beyond Baseball: The Life of Roberto Clemente
http://www.robertoclemente.si.edu

The Official Site of Major League Baseball
http://mlb.mlb.com

Roberto Clemente Sports City
http://www.rcsc21.com

Glossary

citizens: members of a city, town, or other place

earthquake: trembling or shaking of the ground

generous: willing to give to or share with others

Nicaragua: a country in Central America

professional: getting paid to do something instead of doing it as a hobby

selfish: thinking only of oneself

Index